BECAUSE

BECAUSE

A LYRIC MEMOIR

Joshua Mensch

W. W. NORTON & COMPANY

Independent Publishers Since 1923

New York | London

Manufacturing by Quad Graphics, Fairfield
Book design by JAM Design
Production manager: Beth Steidle

ISBN 978-0-393-63522-5

W. W. Norton & Company, Inc., 500 Fifth Avenue, New York, N.Y. 10110
www.wwnorton.com

W. W. Norton & Company Ltd., 15 Carlisle Street, London W1D 3BS

1 2 3 4 5 6 7 8 9 0

BIOGRAPHY
MENSCH

FOR MY PARENTS AND MY SISTERS

CONTENTS

BECAUSE

If I had a thousand tongues,
I could tell a thousand different stories
and all of them would be true;

I

DON

1.

Were it not for a cabin
on Cape Breton Island
with only mist
to break the tree-lined
horizon; were it not
for the two of us:
I was twelve
and together we read
Homer's *Iliad* (not *The Odyssey*) —
though mostly Don
read aloud to me;
his gorgeous voice,
his bathrobe slipping off
his stiff, shiny shins,
his legs like white
radish stalks speckled
with long wiry hairs,
while outside snow
hugged the forest
and a deep fog rose
around the top of the hills,
the snow thick and wet,
ideal for throwing,
and every once in a while
the deep silence
would be interrupted
by a crack like gunfire
as another spruce
snapped under its weight,
bark shrapnel and rolling
sound ricocheting
up the narrow valley

till it reached our meadow,
an eight-sided cabin
with a black stove
that wrapped us in heat
and made our knees itch,
flame-pulsed logs
lighting our limbs with
nail-width lines of blood;

2.

At night he'd read to me
from *The Tracker*,
a chapter at a time,
then tell stories
about his childhood
in Kansas, the endless
fields and grinding
oil wells, floods
that washed away
low-lying houses
and poor people
with them,
his father
whom everyone loved
but him,
his fat mother,
his unhappy sisters;
he'd read to me
and tell me
about my parents
whom he knew
at school in Toronto,
about a woman
named Carmen
and the man
she thought
was the devil,
about his wife, Lorna,
and her head
full of brains, about
the small college
in New Mexico

where the fun
ended when
evil Dean Neidorf
blew a tumor
and had everyone fired,
then sent poison-
pen letters after them:
Don, Lorna,
even my dad, anyone
who wouldn't give
him a blow job;

3.

He'd show me
dirty movies
to inspire me
to try harder
with my body,
for it was truly
impressive
how a guy could shoot
his wad that far —
it didn't matter that
I didn't have a wad
yet but sometimes
a small pearl
of clear lube
appeared at the tip
and he licked
it off, because that
was my accomplishment,
and even though
it wasn't ready yet
he was proud of me;
I knew the names
of animals,
the silhouettes of birds
and the sounds
an engine makes
when climbing up
a hill; I could tell
what gear and how
far away his truck was
and had memorised
the avionic controls

of the fighter jets
that patrolled the coast;
he showed me how
to fashion a battery
from a potato,
how to flood an engine;
I told him
the speed of a bullet
under water,
the speed of the earth
around the sun;
he told me that
floating in space
in orbit
was nothing more
than endless falling;

II

Because

The

Room

Was

Many

Because the room is bright,
    sky-lit, painted white
with a mirrored wall
    and a queen-sized bed;
because it is July,
    hot, and I am half-
undressed already;
    because I let him
undress me the rest of the way, look
    when he tells me to look,
says *look at yourself,*
    aren't you beautiful?;
because I am disgusted
    by the word *beautiful*,
a word for babies and girls,
    a word for sisters,
for my mother;
    because I dive deep
into the bed and let it swallow me,
    and then pull him down
so that it swallows him, too;

Because the room is small, damp   *Times Square, 1991 – Fall*
        cold clinging to our skin
like the dew on the TV,
        every surface wet
from the AC; because outside
        the city is cooking
and we have to keep the television loud
        to drown out
the air conditioner's rattle,
        which won't stop   (we won't stop it)
and wait for night to fall
        so we can finally go out —
Times Square lit up, a glittering
        current of bodies
and glass, where three feet
        in any direction
gets you lost, so he wants
        to hold my hand,
which is embarrassing;
        because he uses the word
kidnapped when I won't let him
        and says, *You don't know*
what some people are capable of —
        and it's true, I don't,
with Don the night is always
        half-awake, when we sleep
he wakes me in my dreams;

Because the room is spare,   *North Grant, 1992 – Spring*
      in an annex to the house
where no one discovers us,
      where no one can hear me
hold my breath then let it go
      — like a river, *like a flood*;

Because the room is not a room   *Meat Cove, 1992 – Summer*
    but a tent near the edge
of a cliff; because the wind won't stop;
    because we wake up
in a pile at the bottom of the tent,
    the stakes nearly out,
the lines taut; because in the dream
    I am having I fail to resist,
or my resistance turns
    into something else;
because it's daybreak, and the birds
    are starting up; because
the other boys are awake and want
    to go whale watching;
because breakfasts need to be made
    and someone calls
his name, so his hand quickens;
    because I come quick
as his hand, which is a hammer;

Because the room is high-ceilinged,   *San Cristóbal, 1993 – Spring*
     airy and loose, cracked
paint flaking from high, white-
     washed walls, crumbling
brick underneath, in one corner
     a pocket of blood-hued
baby spiders; because I smear
     the wall with their tiny
bodies and it looks like I cut
     my hand; because the house
isn't a house but an old colonial
     hotel in San Cristóbal,
a single fan rocking gently
     from the centre of the ceiling,
he lets me sleep, but my fever
     is deep, hallucinatory,
and before long a doctor is called;

1989

Because the room is the room
        on the top floor of a house
in Virginia where we live
        for a year until we move;
because a guest is there,
        and it's not my smelly aunt
but my father's best friend;
        because I am ten
and I have no friends;
        because he says
he wants to be my friend;
        because he invites me
to come to his camp
        and my parents say yes;
because we are moving again
        so *it's really convenient*
for everybody;
        because when I talk
he actually listens
        to what I say;
because he invites me
        up to his room
to sit with him
        on the queen-sized bed
with its light pink spread;
        because the bed
contains the four of us,
        the two that are here
and the two in the mirror;
        because we watch ourselves
being watched by each other
        and he makes it seem
hilarious; because I tell him
        about the girl I like

and for once no one laughs;
    because he asks me
if I want to know
    what a vagina feels like,
and I suddenly really do;
    because he offers
to show me, but only
    if I promise not to tell,
and so I promise, which is easy
    since what he's offering
is what I want, or at least
    what I think will be *amazing*;
because when it happens
    I am literally amazed;
because his hand moves faster
    than any hand should move
it's like I'm leaving the earth,
    like the earth is not
a real thing anymore;
    because it's over
as soon as it starts,
    and when it burns,
he tells me *this pain is the sharpest*
    part of pleasure;
because you glimpse yourself
    in the mirror,
sprawled across the lap
    of a bearded man
whose hands grace your neck,
    your legs, your chest;
because where there was skin
    now there is rupture,
and no one can see it but you,
    so your promise

must be the glue
     that binds this new body
to the rest of you;
     because dinner is ready
and it's time to move;
     because your mother
is calling you; because your
     father is calling you;
because it's time to move;

Because the room is the cabin   *Air Atlantic, 1989 – Summer*
        of a plane that carries
me to him, clouds falling up
        like rain in reverse
as the plane descends; because
        the room is an island
where Don is waiting; because
        the fog is heavy and
the ground arrives with a bump,
        trees materialising
out of the mist and the slick
        runway screaming back
as its engines grind to a halt
        in Sydney, Cape Breton
Island, a three-hour drive
        from the Margaree Valley
where Don's camp nests
        deep in the hills that ring
the valley floor, a place called
        Forest Glen, far away
from electricity and cars, parents
        and their rules, where
boys can run naked and play
        Indian; because for months
this was all I looked forward to,
        and the fifteen minutes
it takes the plane to come to a stop
        on the tarmac, the extra five
to grab my backpack
        and file down the narrow
aisle to the door, descend the steps
        to the wet asphalt
and walk the remaining yards
        to the terminal where

Don waits on an orange seat
        studying a map of the island,
half a dozen boys slouched
        about him like restless
dogs, ends in a moment of silence;
        because arrival is always
accompanied by silence; because
        I am new to this camp
and the others clearly aren't;
        because still more
are coming, which means more
        waiting, more staring
at my feet, more hands to shake;

Because the room is the tent that   *Fishing Cove, 1989 – Summer*
        I built three times
to get it right, twisting each pole
        through its proper hoop;
because I had to carry this
        tent *and* my own food *and*
my own water *and* my own wet
        clothes twelve kilometres
through a damp jungle of ferns,
        grass and fiddleheads,
sinking into the soft moss between
        thickets of black spruce;
because I actually crapped myself
        along the way and now
there's a picture of me holding
        my stained underwear
on a stick, with G. and M. grinning
        beside me; because this
is the kind of accident Don finds
        unbearably cute (of course
I tried to hide it under a bush,
        and of course G. ratted
me out — *whatever you pack in*
        you have to pack out);
because Fishing Cove is gorgeous
        and remote, *truly unspoiled*;
because the first thing fifteen boys
        do in an unspoiled place
is try to spoil it, so we play tag
        loudly and pee in the river
and bury our trash when Don is
        not looking; because
I'm finally making friends
        and I want to be the baddest

of them all, so I throw
      my shitty underwear
into the fire, where it stinks like a
      smokey fart; because
Don wants me to stay with him
      but G. and M. and K.
and R. want to be with him, too,
      so in the end we pile up
together; because we find bear prints
      in the mud around our
campsite the next morning and beg
      Don to let us track it;
because for the last two weeks
      we've been hard at work
building bows and arrows
      and believe we have
what it takes to catch a bear;
      because we're all secretly
relieved when Don forbids us
      from doing anything
that could get him sued;
      because this is camp life,
loud and rowdy and gross,
      and for once, we are free
to pretend we are not afraid
      of the dark — out here,
where the stars spread their milk
      across the sky,
every shadow is a predator,
      but Don always keeps us
safe by his side;

Because the room is made of wood,   *Forest Glen, 1989 – Summer*
    whole logs stripped and stacked
and joined to form an octagon;
    because it is an hour's hike
from the nearest house; because it's
    so dark at night my eyes
can't adjust no matter how hard
    I try; because we aren't
alone — maybe half a dozen boys,
    some my age, most a bit
older, are passed out on the floor
    in their sleeping bags,
black lumps to be felt with a foot,
    verified by a snore;
because the air is thick
    and my heart jumps
until all I hear is blood;
    because we've been playing
this game for weeks, the game
    in which we play uncovered,
right in front of everyone,
    but have to be quiet;

1990

Because the room is not a room   *St. Andrews JHS, 1990 – Fall*
    but a bathroom stall where
your enemies have installed you
    (or, rather, re-installed
you) for the fifth day in a row;
    because your stupid nose
is bleeding like an open faucet
    (it does this randomly)
and you've already clogged the toilet
    with an entire roll
of toilet paper; because the bowl
    is overflowing now
and soon there'll be shrieks
    from the girls doing their
own hiding in neighbouring stalls;
    because this is the school
you go to, where you eat lunch
    in the library, where it's quiet,
discreetly stuffing down the sandwich
    your father made for you;
because you can't stay here forever —
    when the bell rings
there is still the long hallway,
    its endless rows of lockers;

Because the room is not a room
    but a phone call,
the principal at my school
    has concerns,
ran a background check
    and turned up reports
from a camp where Don worked
    ten years before,
alleging impropriety with
    children, mostly minors
from broken homes — *retribution,*
    Don said later,
for his complaints that the kids
    weren't being fed enough,
weren't given clean clothes
    (*You know me,* he said,
I'm always fighting for the interests
    of our youngest citizens);
because Don is my father's best
    friend, and mine, too;
because school sucks;
    because Don doesn't ask
for more than the cost of my keep
    to homeschool me;
because I've already been in his care,
    and deny everything
when my father quizzes me
    about his behaviour,
asks if Don has ever touched me
    down there; because I beg
to go; because Don's cabin is quiet,
    and we can read Plato
and track animals through the forest;
    because he likes me,

30

which is really nice of him;
     because of history,
which goes back forever
     between friends; because
even when I ask him about it
     later, say, *Don, do you*
do this to the others, too? he looks
     shocked and says
No, no, there's only you, Oh god,
     there's only you;

Because the room is a window
    seat on a bus grinding
against snow and blowing winds
    up the 401
to Cape Breton Island where Don
    is waiting to pick me up;
because the causeway is piled
    with ice and buried cars;
because there's music playing,
    a tinny AM radio tuned
in to a Nashville hit, which fades
    in and out of the static;
because the wind outside throws
    its own static across
the road in sheets so thick
    the bus is forced to crawl,
stop, threaten not to make it,
    which would mean going back
to my father, who will say, *I'm sorry,*
    you can't miss more school;
because even one more day
    at school would kill me;
because the bus finally makes it,
    and seeing Don standing
under the port next to his van
    floods me with relief;
because his wife, Lorna, is with him
    and she is *so happy*
to see me, they *won't be alone*
    this winter after all
and she has so much to teach me
    about the earth, the
environment, *the building blocks*
    of the natural world;

because Don couldn't *not* let her
        come along, we have
shopping to do and she wants to
        buy her own things;
because Don doesn't want to
        answer my questions
while she's around, so I have
        to hold my tongue,
which is burning; because I can't
        even wait until Lorna
rounds the corner with the first
        load of groceries to
blurt out a word I've never used
        before, *pedophile*, a word
that sounds like what it means;
        because he tells me
my understanding of its meaning
        is wrong, *or not wrong*
but imprecise; because what he feels
        is not *attraction* but
fondness; because *who is society*
        to tell us what we can
and can't do with our own bodies?;
        because *it* is not something
most people *understand*; because
        I want to understand
and react badly when he tells me
        to stop, to *settle down*;
because it's time to take the rest
        of the groceries inside
and then there's dinner to make;
        because it takes ages
for Lorna to finally retire
        to her own small cabin

fifty metres down the road,
        a replica of Thoreau's
at Walden Pond surrounded
        by a grove of poplar
and birch, with a large window
        facing the road;
because society thinks it can
        regulate our desires;
because as soon as we're alone
        we are naked, face-to-face
on the Big Bed, a kerosene lamp
        on an unopened book
between us, which makes his eyes
        twinkle and his skin glow
like a source of heat; because
        I'm tired of hugging
my knees; because when he asks,
        Doesn't it feel good? and
Why should you or I be ashamed of it?,
        I don't really have
an answer; because his logic
        seems completely solid;
because *I* let *him* take things
        further than before,
let him show me how
        he does it to himself;

Because the room is a one-room
    cabin with a bed,
a desk and a step ladder that
    leads up to a small loft
where Lorna keeps her books,
    no toilet, not even
a sink with running water
    to wash her face,
so she has to bathe in the house;
    because I have
to stay upstairs when Lorna
    is naked and peek
through the cracks in the floor
    to see what she
looks like; because the floor
    is made of a single
layer of hardwood, wide panels
    hewn from trees
that stood where Don cleared
    the land to build
his house; because Lorna's breasts
    are larger and fuller
than I expected from her shirt,
    heavy, white balloons
hanging gracefully from her chest
    as she leans over
with a towel to dry a leg;
    because I shuffle
from gap to gap to watch her
    as she crosses the room;
because I imagine her
    coming upstairs
instead of Don, or at least
    joining us; because she says,

Josh! I hope you're not peeking and
        I can hear you breathing
through the cracks, so I scramble
        off the floor, almost
knocking a bookshelf over;
        because Don comes up
fifteen minutes later to tell me
        tonight he's going
to Lorna's, so I have to spend
        the next few hours
alone, terrified both of the dark
        upstairs, and of being
seen by marauders in the light
        of the kitchen below,
where there is no place to hide
        from anyone; because
when Don returns I am almost out
        of breath with relief
yet deny it vehemently when he
        teases me for being
scared; because the whole point
        of me being here
is to not be afraid,
        and it embarrasses me
that I am not truly wild
        the way I pretend to be,
and when Lorna later calls me
        coureur des bois—
runner of the woods, I feel ashamed
        that even a walk
to the chicken coop, or down
        to the river, makes me
want to run in fear of what might
        try to get me; because

I never venture into the forest
        alone like E., the boy
from the valley who disappears
        for days at a time
just to be alone, who emerges
        unscathed by the dark
and sometimes even
        bearing a trophy,
a rabbit or a grouse, which Don
        strips and spices
and roasts with root vegetables
        from the cellar,
which I fetch by climbing down
        through a small trapdoor
in the middle of the floor,
        terrified of what
might happen if it closed;

Because the room is the top floor
    of the cabin where we
are completely alone for the first
    time ever, no other kids,
Lorna fifty metres away in her *retreat*
    and no neighbours
for five miles in the only direction
    possible to travel by road;
because I've just completed my first
    assignment for Don's
"class," three questions on Plato's
    Ion (1. he was a poet,
2. he couldn't defend his verse,
    3. he must have been
blessed by forces larger than himself),
    which leads to more
questions (1. was he a real poet
    or merely a performer
of someone else's words?
    2. what wisdom does
poetry express that plainspoken
    knowledge cannot
through logic deduce?); because
    math class is Chapter 1
of Euclid's proofs; because
    the books are old, worn
with study; because Don turns on
    the generator as soon
as the lesson is over so we
    can watch *Dead Poets*
Society on VHS starring Don
    as Robin Williams and me
as the deep-feeling guy who dies
    at the end (which

prompts me to ask: *Why*
        would someone kill himself
just to get back at his dad?)
        until the gas runs out;
because the generator can
        only run for two hours
max on a single tank of gas,
        so we're lucky we make it
to the credits before the television
        blacks out, along with
the room; because matches
        are found by groping hands
and a single candle is lit,
        a slim embryo of light
in a wooden womb, *a chiaroscuro:*
        Man and Boy on Bed,
Don's stack of *Hustlers* no longer
        hidden but just out
of reach, so he says, *Go ahead,*
        take a look; because
Don wants to use his mouth
        this time, reminds me
that I promised to let him *once*
        we got to know each other
a little more; because I once used
        the phrase he used
with me the first time I asked him
        what the inside of a girl
felt like, which was the first time
        we met and his hand
was covered in my sister's lotion,
        which he slathered
all over my chest and down
        my legs, wherever my skin

was exposed; because my answer
        is still *no* — and I'm not
sure why it's such a big deal
        but now it's a matter
of principle; because he tries
        to lower his head
anyway, so I push at his scalp, pull
        his thinning hair away;
because he turns his back to me
        and I feel bad for him,
so I pull him back around but keep
        my belly facedown
so all he can tickle is my rump
        until I pass out, wake up
uncovered with the winter sun
        licking me, bright,
without heat;

Because the room is a cabin   *Forest Glen, 1990 – Winter*
          surrounded by frost-
bitten trees, where torrents
          of white gather
in furious gusts, get tangled
          in branches or ram
themselves into trunks; because
          the wind is literally
howling at the walls where
          Lorna and I sit
sipping tea among scattered
          clothes, dirty cups
and jars of pee, waiting for the
          gale to pass;
because the outhouse is fifty
          metres away and
outside the wind whips ice
          into our faces;
because it is better to sleep
          with the tang of urine
than to go outside and fight
          the blowing snow
just to relieve some tension;
          because the room
is thick with incense, bunches
          of lavender hang
from rafters absorbing smoke
          from the tiny cones
that smoulder and ossify in
          a bowl on Lorna's desk,
become fragile dust that explodes
          and settles on the sill
of the frost-covered window
          every time one of us

sneezes or coughs; because it is
    deep winter, *inviting*
meditation and sleep; because Don
    is out with J., our new
student (taken on for the spring)
    getting groceries
and making phone calls from
    the old rotary telephone
in the schoolhouse:
    J. to his mother in
Montreal, Don to his tax advisor;
    because Lorna sings
the song of my name to me:
    my name fought a battle
and the walls *came a-tumbling down*;
    because it wasn't his horn
that felled the city but his eyes —
    through Joshua's eyes
God saw what Jericho had become
    and saw fit to shatter it;
because to see is to devastate;
    because Lorna believes
that science is the study of life,
    and that *to study life*
you have to look at life —
    only in the natural world
can the answer be found; because
    Lorna had the potential
to turn the world of cell biology
    upside down, and when
Don tells me later that he wrote
    Lorna's dissertation

after she had a nervous break-
    down, he makes sure
to point out that *the core research*
    was hers; because Lorna
believes *it's not the observation of things*
    but their beings,
their being-ness that clues us in
    to dimensions that exist
beyond our single slice of the universe;
    because Lorna wants
to teach me how to meditate,
    how to block out thought
but not the senses, so that I, too, can
    feel the other bodies
I have lived in; because I imagine
    my previous lives
stacked like sheets of paper,
    on each one *a story*
of who you were and how you got here;
    because I beg Lorna
to ask about me the next time
    she talks to the *Voice*
of Light, a woman in San Antonio,
    Texas, whom Lorna calls
every few months to get patched
    through to God;
because God is not *a man*
    but *a highway* along
which all souls travel, occasionally
    falling off and dropping
into lives like the ones we're in
    right now; because,

43

sometimes, the souls of lovers
    dive off the side
of the highway, one chasing
    the other so that
they can be together longer,
    only to end up brothers
or on opposite sides of a war;

1991

Because the room is a *theatre*
  where *the last war ever*
is taking place, *Desert Storm,*
   Stormin' Norman,
Colin Powell and *a sober ex-vice-*
   president whom Don
says *controls things quietly*, pushing
  buttons to kill Iraqis,
thousands of them at a time,
  while the *Yanks*
and the French, the dozens of other
  countries *there for show*
die exclusively by *friendly fire*,
  a few at a time; because
I proclaim this war to be the last
  one ever, and Lorna
agrees with me; because
  You don't have to worry
about who will win, the stakes are so
  uneven; because every
town in America has yellow ribbons
  tied to their trees
and awnings and porch pillars,
  tied to signs saying
Support Our Troops and *Not One Life*
  though none of *our boys*
it seems are in any real danger
  except from themselves
and the weather; because it's so cold
  I can't even imagine
the heat of a desert; because
  the last time we protested
the country almost shattered (Don);
  because *we've*

been here before, it was the same
    in Athens (Lorna);
because Lorna and Don were there,
    two athletes, friends,
men competing against each other
    and they're still trying
to finish their race after all these
    years; because I was
a monk in my past life (she asked!)
    and before that a swami
in India, which is disappointing;
    because the *Voice of Light*
thinks my purpose in life is to
    reconcile Christianity
with Reincarnation, neither of which
    strikes me as particularly
interesting; because I'd rather ask her
    silly questions like
what if a dinosaur in the year minus
    2 million came back
as a house cat on a spaceship
    in the year 2020; because
she gives disappointing answers
    like *Souls are God's*
experiments in embodiment and
    Our form is no accident
which I take to mean God won't
    bring me back as an eagle,
or even a wolf, even if I ask him to;
    because according to
Lorna I don't actually have other lives,
    just one continuous life
that somehow keeps going in spite
    of my many bodies;

because *each of our lives happens*
    out of order
but it's not like time travel, it's that
    time doesn't exist
in the spiritual dimension; because
    time and space apply
to physical bodies, but *the universe*
    is much more than that;
because in the spiritual dimension
    time is one and so
it's not really like a highway at all
    but like a parking lot,
all you have to do to get a new life
    is walk to the edge
and jump off;

Because the room is not a room   _Forest Glen, 1991 – Spring_
    but an entire house and
Don and I are the only ones in it;
    because it is still winter,
and the black cast-iron stove
    doubles as a fireplace,
around which both of us shiver;
    because it is early morning
and the hills are a mosaic
    of white-robed spruce
rolled in snow like rounds
    of cotton glass, so soft
I imagine myself a giant
    rolling over them;
because that which keeps you warm
    also cuts; because Don
insists we lie naked together,
    for shared bodily warmth,
and my body is small enough to be
    enfolded in his arms;
because his cock gets in the way,
    presses against the small
of my back and it annoys me;
    because I say so, and he
turns away and takes the blankets
    with him; because I
pull him back; because soon
    enough it is morning,
there's a fire roaring in the stove
    downstairs, its thick,
black pipes shuddering from the
    sudden heat, and tea,
blistering hot even with mittens,
    is already whistling

e feather in his hair,
ays, *See, now*
feel better? and asks
wants to go into town
nd buy candy
general store?;

in the kettle; because this is
    the best place in the world
during the day when things are normal,
    a wilderness without
judgement, only the usual dangers;
    because we all know
what happens to a child lost
    in a forest at night;

Because the room is not a room   *Forest Glen, 1991 – Spring*
     but a place where many
things happen — a room full of books,
     National Geographics
stacked five deep along one wall,
     tiny, dusty objects from
Don's travels around the world,
     gods in all shapes and
sizes in wood and onyx, leathered
     flesh and mounted fur;
because I have nothing to do
     but read and it's still
just the two of us together —
     when the others come
camp will start and my life
     will go back to normal;
because it is spring, almost
     summer, and after that
I will have to go back to school
     where rules are taught
and knowledge is ruined;
     because I feel
incredibly smart having heard
     Don read the entire
Iliad aloud, having read Plato
     myself, wrapping
a white sheet over my torso,
     having dressed
as a Native American
     in a leather thong
of my own making, which Don
     finds cute so he takes
a picture, which I plan to burn
     as soon as it is developed;

Because the room is a field
     surrounded by trees
where your enemies are waiting
     because this is *war*
and the red band on your arm
     tells everyone else
who you are; because the arrow
     tip is blunt, but the bow
is strong, you made it that way;
     because the game
is to get the blue bandana from
     the other team's fort
on the other side of those trees
     so you circle around
and catch the blond boy hiding
     behind a bush, tap
him with your bow so he lies
     dead, no peal of horror;
because you're close enough
     to capture your prize,
so you make a run for it but get
     tapped by R., which means
you're dead, which infuriates
     you; because you're dead
and you lie on the ground star
     up at the trees waiting
for Don's whistle; because this
     is how enemies are made
and afterwards a fight breaks
     so Don makes us sit
in a circle with a talking feath
     because all manner of
complaints come out, and wh
     Don's turn comes

he puts
     an
don't we
     W
tomorro
     at t

Because there's nothing so satisfying   *Leesburg, 1991 – Fall*
    as ripping apart your
own skin, watching layer after
    layer peel away until
even pain has no origin; because
    the poison has seeped
all over your hands, spread to your
    legs, your arms, your chest,
covered your crotch so that it burns
    even worse than the rest;
because you're visiting your mother
    before school starts
and it only took you one day
    to wander into a patch
of poison ivy and now your trip
    is ruined: your face,
your neck, a splotchy mess, so you
    can't even go outside;
because you can't keep your hands
    out of your pants; because
strangely, the inflamed flesh
    makes you aroused,
so you scratch one itch to relieve
    the other; because
the doctor chuckles when he sees
    your penis, swollen
beyond belief, and prescribes a cream
    to relieve the swelling,
but it's too late, you've already
    refined your technique
and another itch persists
    despite the return

to normal dimensions —
    and interestingly,
your method is just like Don's,
    a two-finger pinch,
though you lack his stamina
    in the wrist;

1992

Because the room is a one-room   *Margaree Valley, 1992 – Summer*
    schoolhouse where Don
keeps a telephone and bicycles
    and a large fast-freezer
filled with boxes of Popsicles,
    blocks of meat
and bags of frozen green beans
    five miles from the cabin
in the woods where he teaches us
    to track animals and build
sweat lodges and stretch deerskin
    into drums, how to plane
wood by hand to make strong bows
    and which twigs to strip
to make the straightest arrows;
    because there are more
abandoned cabins in these hills
    than inhabited ones,
so you learn to find your own;
    because to find the perfect arrow
is to shoot it, to calculate the wind,
    to make a lean-to out of twigs
and leaves and a long spine post
    heaved over a rock,
to build a fire and a heat reflector,
    to play your drum in time
with the others, and to know
    what roots to pick
and which ferns are edible,
    each morning a hunt
for what we might eat at lunch,
    and in the winter, to read,
to think, to keep warm at night;

Because the room is not a room   *Forest Glen, 1992 – Summer*
     but a small clearing deep
in the forest halfway up
     the mountain that rises
behind our cabin; because I am
     alone here, having hiked
farther into the hills behind
     Don's cabin than I've dared
to before; because I didn't
     tell anyone at camp
where I was going, I could stay
     out here all night, maybe
even forever, and not see another
     person again; because
even this lost I know I'm not alone,
     I feel the eyes of animals
upon me, feel even the eyes
     of old Indian ghosts;
because my skin is untempered
     by the weather, my spirit
untested by a night without walls,
     without a roof, without
blankets, with only the fire
     I'd have to make myself,
with no one else, I question
     my ability to survive,
and it annoys me; because this
     is a story I read to myself:
a young brave who goes to the top
     of a mountain for three
days and three nights to become
     a man; who has visions,
who talks to his spirit animal,
     who soars over his village

in the kettle; because this is
 the best place in the world
during the day when things are normal,
 a wilderness without
judgement, only the usual dangers;
 because we all know
what happens to a child lost
 in a forest at night;

Because the room is not a room   *Forest Glen, 1991 – Spring*
        but a place where many
things happen — a room full of books,
        National Geographics
stacked five deep along one wall,
        tiny, dusty objects from
Don's travels around the world,
        gods in all shapes and
sizes in wood and onyx, leathered
        flesh and mounted fur;
because I have nothing to do
        but read and it's still
just the two of us together —
        when the others come
camp will start and my life
        will go back to normal;
because it is spring, almost
        summer, and after that
I will have to go back to school
        where rules are taught
and knowledge is ruined;
        because I feel
incredibly smart having heard
        Don read the entire
Iliad aloud, having read Plato
        myself, wrapping
a white sheet over my torso,
        having dressed
as a Native American
        in a leather thong
of my own making, which Don
        finds cute so he takes
a picture, which I plan to burn
        as soon as it is developed;

Because the room is a field   *Forest Glen, 1991 – Summer*
    surrounded by trees
where your enemies are waiting;
    because this is *war*
and the red band on your arm
    tells everyone else
who you are; because the arrow
    tip is blunt, but the bow
is strong, you made it that way;
    because the game
is to get the blue bandana from
    the other team's fort
on the other side of those trees,
    so you circle around
and catch the blond boy hiding
    behind a bush, tap
him with your bow so he lies down
    dead, no peal of horror;
because you're close enough
    to capture your prize,
so you make a run for it but get
    tapped by R., which means
you're dead, which infuriates
    you; because you're dead
and you lie on the ground staring
    up at the trees waiting
for Don's whistle; because this
    is how enemies are made,
and afterwards a fight breaks out,
    so Don makes us sit
in a circle with a talking feather;
    because all manner of
complaints come out, and when
    Don's turn comes

he puts the feather in his hair,
        and says, *See, now*
don't we all feel better? and asks
        Who wants to go into town
tomorrow and buy candy
        at the general store?;

Because there's nothing so satisfying *Leesburg, 1991 – Fall*
    as ripping apart your
own skin, watching layer after
    layer peel away until
even pain has no origin; because
    the poison has seeped
all over your hands, spread to your
    legs, your arms, your chest,
covered your crotch so that it burns
    even worse than the rest;
because you're visiting your mother
    before school starts
and it only took you one day
    to wander into a patch
of poison ivy and now your trip
    is ruined: your face,
your neck, a splotchy mess, so you
    can't even go outside;
because you can't keep your hands
    out of your pants; because
strangely, the inflamed flesh
    makes you aroused,
so you scratch one itch to relieve
    the other; because
the doctor chuckles when he sees
    your penis, swollen
beyond belief, and prescribes a cream
    to relieve the swelling,
but it's too late, you've already
    refined your technique
and another itch persists
    despite the return

to normal dimensions —
  and interestingly,
your method is just like Don's,
  a two-finger pinch,
though you lack his stamina
  in the wrist;

1992

Because the room is a one-room   *Margaree Valley, 1992 – Summer*
    schoolhouse where Don
keeps a telephone and bicycles
    and a large fast-freezer
filled with boxes of Popsicles,
    blocks of meat
and bags of frozen green beans
    five miles from the cabin
in the woods where he teaches us
    to track animals and build
sweat lodges and stretch deerskin
    into drums, how to plane
wood by hand to make strong bows
    and which twigs to strip
to make the straightest arrows;
    because there are more
abandoned cabins in these hills
    than inhabited ones,
so you learn to find your own;
    because to find the perfect arrow
is to shoot it, to calculate the wind,
    to make a lean-to out of twigs
and leaves and a long spine post
    heaved over a rock,
to build a fire and a heat reflector,
    to play your drum in time
with the others, and to know
    what roots to pick
and which ferns are edible,
    each morning a hunt
for what we might eat at lunch,
    and in the winter, to read,
to think, to keep warm at night;

Because the room is not a room   *Forest Glen, 1992 – Summer*
        but a small clearing deep
in the forest halfway up
        the mountain that rises
behind our cabin; because I am
        alone here, having hiked
farther into the hills behind
        Don's cabin than I've dared
to before; because I didn't
        tell anyone at camp
where I was going, I could stay
        out here all night, maybe
even forever, and not see another
        person again; because
even this lost I know I'm not alone,
        I feel the eyes of animals
upon me, feel even the eyes
        of old Indian ghosts;
because my skin is untempered
        by the weather, my spirit
untested by a night without walls,
        without a roof, without
blankets, with only the fire
        I'd have to make myself,
with no one else, I question
        my ability to survive,
and it annoys me; because this
        is a story I read to myself:
a young brave who goes to the top
        of a mountain for three
days and three nights to become
        a man; who has visions,
who talks to his spirit animal,
        who soars over his village

and sees his sisters down by the
        river and his mother
hard at work, who sees the woman
        he will marry and the
child they will have together,
        who will be his apple,
who sees his entire future and how
        short the path is, both
behind him and ahead of him,
        and resolves to live all of it,
no matter what happens to him;
        because it is a child's
story, but I still want to be in it;
        because there is peace
in these woods, too, and when I close
        my eyes I can hear the trees
whispering, can hear insects
        chewing and trunks creaking
and the drumbeat of birds flitting
        through the underbrush;
because I wait until the late,
        low sun's fingers ignite
the forest's litter, setting fire
        to carpets of moss,
blazing fallen logs and crumbling
        stumps, until the ferns
glimmer like fingered parasols,
        lighting even me
with an ember of flame; because
        this is the moment
I need to become someone else;
        because time doesn't stand
still, and neither does the sun;
        because soon it will be

dark and difficult to find my way
    back; because the forest
is growing denser and scarier
    even as the sky breaks
into colors more beautiful than any
    I've ever seen before;
because the sky's so gorgeous
    I can't look away, can't
bring myself to climb back down
    the boulder that lets me
see clear across the valley;
    because I want to stay,
I need this vision, I need to know
    what my spirit animal
looks like, what my future has to say;
    because I sit on that rock
until the sun crashes down
    into its own dirty rainbow
and the hills across from me go black;

Because the room is a circle of light   *Forest Glen, 1992 – Summer*
    where two weeks later
I am surrounded by deepest darkness;
    because the fire is low,
so I stoke it and toss more
    leaves on it to make it
rise up and glow; because I've made
    this fire myself; because
I will spend the next two nights
    down by the river,
waiting for my vision to appear;
    because I can hear
the river roaring, unstoppable
    on its way to the sea;
because I am thirsty; because
    I really have to pee;
because I am too afraid to venture
    into what I cannot see;
because I need this fire
    to ward off those
who would eat me; because I want
    a vision, but visions
don't come to those who aren't free
    of their bodies; because
I am hungry, my bag of nuts
    reduced to dust which I lick
until the plastic rips; because
    I can't bring myself to
extinguish the fire while I sleep,
    and so I wake up cold
to still-warm cinders and a burn-
    hole in my sleeping bag;
because the light this early has
    no source, it will be hours

before the sun crests the lowest
    hill and dries the dew
that covers every leaf and blade
    of grass in this valley;
because the birds will not wait
    for the sun to grace the trees
to flood the forest with their
    cacophony; because
the mosquitos have already had
    their way with my body,
and now the black flies
    are coming for their due;
because this is the first part
    of my vision quest —
I have to survive beyond my body
    in order to see what
my eyes won't allow me; because
    two days later, dizzy
with hunger, I will see a hawk
    resting on the lowest branch
of the closest tree; because it doesn't
    move when I don't move;
because it disappears when I do;

Because the room is not a room
    but a hillside with a
clear view of the only raincloud
    in the sky, a bulbous
monstrosity with a crimson cap
    and a swollen purple
belly rimmed by a belt of rich
    desert gold from all
the dust kicked up around it;
    because it is the single
most beautiful thing I have ever
    seen and I want Don
to stop watching it with me;
    because we were
almost caught the night before;
    because Don wanted us
to be alone so we could *do more*;
    because it got so cold
we had no choice but to zip
    our sleeping bags together
and strip off all our clothes
    for *shared bodily warmth*;
because the next morning
    a forest ranger found us,
huddled together like lovers,
    and hollered us awake
from his truck, giving us just
    enough time to haul on
our underwear and pants,
    and for Don to come up
with a story about how his
    flashlight got lost and
we couldn't find our way back
    to the campsite so we

had to build a fire — *yes, we know*
       we're not supposed to —
and so fire becomes the issue,
       how clever;
because Don broke the rules,
       our rule was always
no means no and yet I woke up
       with his mouth around me
for the third time this trip;
       because he *can't help* himself
and is always contrite, so it seems
       better to focus on
what he will buy me for breakfast;

1993

Because the room is a beach hut
    in Mexico that takes us
three hours to reach by bus;
    because we're already
sick of each other, with S. and J.,
    Don's two students,
already at one another's throats
    and Don's talking
feather incapable of doing
    anything to resolve it;
because J. can't keep his hands off
    S. at night and S. can't
stop bitching about it; because
    to keep the peace
I offer to share my bed with J.,
    even though I hate
the way he smells, that little-kid
    stink — gooey, sweet;
because he wants to feel me up
    and I finally let him;
because I let him get me off
    one night and again
the next, until I've had enough
    of it; because I've had
enough of it but Don hasn't,
    wants to see for himself
what we do at night; because
    one day we return
from the beach to find all the beds
    pushed together,
which sends me into a rage
    at the three of them;
because I wander the beach alone
    and run into the woman

I met earlier, an entomologist
      twenty years my senior
who offered to give me a lesson
      in *human anatomy*
and removed her top just as Don
      called me away;
because the woman is an expert
      in the mating habits
of insects and lays out
      an impressive collection
of beetles and flies on the sand,
      today's catch,
and lets me touch each one;
      because I hoped
my sunglasses were dark enough
      to stop her eyes from
seeing me staring at her breasts;
      because I couldn't
stop staring at her breasts
      and she finally
called me out on it, but in the
      most gentle way,
telling me not to be ashamed,
      it's ok to watch,
and later, *it's ok to touch;*
      because Don suddenly
can't stand any trysts that might
      make me *a man,*
so we pack up and go to San
      Cristóbal a day early;
because all I want is to march
      insects between her
breasts and squeeze her nipples
      till milk comes

pouring out (or so I imagine it);
    because I get bitchy
and kick J. out of my bed
    that night, telling Don
I'm not sharing anymore;
    because Don thinks he can
calm me with his mouth;
    because I push him
away at first but finally give in;
    because the woman's
skin is soft and smells nice
    and Don smells of
armpit, crotch, and unwashed
    scalp, like fish guts;
because the tickle of his beard
    makes it take forever
and by the end of it his mouth
    is in pain (*good*, I think)
because J., whose mouth is soft,
    gets tired quicker
than I can come; because I can't
    come anymore
with my hand or anyone else's;
    because for some reason
my body and my imagination
    won't work together,
all I see are hands and mouths
    and a body I don't want;

Because the room is a bathroom   *San Cristóbal, 1993 – Spring*
     in an old colonial hotel
with tiny tiles arranged in a drunk
     mosaic, varying shades
of blue with no discernible pattern;
     because my fever has
not yet reached its pitch and my
     delirium is merely
building; because Don thinks
     I can ride it out,
and doesn't call a doctor until
     the third night;
because I am hallucinating —
     blocks of time
come at me like massive, three-
     dimensional cubes,
one per flick of the radio clock,
     till sunlight breaks
through the frosted glass
     and Don wakes up
and lifts me off the floor;
     because I ordered
the hamburger at the "western"
     café next to the old
colonial hotel; because
     the burger came with
crisp, fresh lettuce, freshly cut
     onions and a tomato
still beaded with the water
     it had been rinsed in;
because the water, drunk by half
     a million people a day,
is not safe to drink unless you
     grew up with it;

because at fourteen I am totally
        out of my element,
and I say horrible things to Don
        whenever he crosses me,
which is almost always;
        because I imagine
the horrible things that might
        happen to him
and think of ways to make them
        happen; because I wake
in a fever to find Don's wrist
        flailing at my hips;
because Don is drenched in sweat
        and smells like a man
who doesn't know how to bathe;
        because the hard knocking
of his hand against my pelvis
        shakes me awake,
and I push him away so violently
        he hits his head on the
bed frame and comes back bleeding
        from his scalp; because
it feels good, almost victorious,
        to have hurt him so badly;

Because the room is an Aztec
    panic room where
sacrificed children were bound
    with rope and had
their hearts cut out then burned
    in cups of flames,
Temple of Doom style;
    because I won't talk
to him, won't talk to anyone now
    and he declares he's
had enough, says, *I'm sick*
    of this shit and *I give up*;
because I say, *give up what?*
    then hate him
and shut him out even more;
    because he feels
wronged, says,
    How many other
teenagers have someone who
    will suck their cock
on command?
    and it shocks me,
he has never referred to it
    so coarsely before,
not a *beautiful organ*, or
    a *part of your body*
but a *cock*; because everything
    that was once forbidden
is now *commonplace*, like
    the legs of a piano,
bare as a mirror after a death;
    because he asked
me once, *Why is any of this*
    taboo?; because when

we get back to the hotel I am
        no longer a nice young
man but a *mean kid* and it's true,
        I don't really care
about Don, or the other boys,
        because we're all
just trying to survive each other
        any way we can;

Because the room is his old room
	in the house where he
grew up; because it contains
	the wreckage of his younger
self, boxes filled with pictures,
	graded papers, report cards,
passport photos in which only
	his mouth is recognizable;
because his mother insists his
	father was a gentle man;
because Don insists his father
	was not, so the truth
of who his father was and what
	he may have done
is rather obscured;
	because it is summer again
and I just want to be outside
	with the others,
I don't care if a storm is coming;
	because he insists
I stay with him at his mother's
	and not at his sister's
like everyone else;
	because I am older now,
and angry enough to kill him;
	because his niece
does things to the others
	I've only heard about
and offers to do them to me, too,
	but Don won't let me
spend the night at her house;
	because I try to make it
over there on my own and get
	caught in a storm

so terrible it makes the news,
    and when Don finally
finds me hiding beneath a tree
    he puts his arm
around me, takes my bike
    and loads it onto the rack
and puts a towel on my neck;
    because I just wanted
to get off, with anyone, it hardly
    mattered who; because,
for once, he offers me money,
    and so I finally cave,
fuck him
    the way he wants me to;

Because the room is the deck
    of a house belonging
to Don's old friends who are also
    my parents' old friends,
who love him and won't believe
    the charges that will
be leveled against him, who will
    write letters on his behalf
saying *Don truly loves children*;
    because Don babysat
their own children back when
    all of us lived here
in this perpetual amber light
    under which everything
is beautiful; because Don is still
    a hero to everyone;
because he is still considered sane
    and hasn't lost
his shit yet, though his face,
    if you look closely,
betrays the strain; because he still
    bothers to be charming,
to be the *good old Don* who might
    not have the academic
acuity of his friends, but whose
    gift for friendship they
can only marvel at — *how easily*
    troubled boys take to him,
how quickly they mature
    under his attention,
how confident they are, how
    authoritative they become
in matters of the body and the mind;
    because it's dinnertime —

tonight we will eat burritos
        with red and green
chile and afterwards sleep
        under the stars;
because I am determined
        to sleep alone tonight,
but Don insists I sleep next to him;
        because to protest
is to call attention to myself;
        because I can tell
he is trying desperately
        to keep his hands off
the others; because he is nearing
        the end of his ability
to maintain his fiction;
        because I *understand*,
I am *the important one*,
        the only one;

Because the room is the entire
        second floor of the cabin
where everyone sleeps together
        and downstairs is the place
where everyone eats and it is
        the most normal place
in the world until you visit,
        already fifteen and
not really surprised that Don
        can't keep it together
anymore; because everything
        is unbelievably
fucked up now, he isn't even
        trying to hide it — one kid,
a husky, powerful twelve-year-old,
        is so giddy he pulls
out his willy at the table,
        and later, complaints
spill out over the talking feather —
        in this way, they
appeal to me for help; because
        I am now the oldest,
the one who can say *fuck you*
        to Don, *so can you please*
tell him to stop?;
        because I take him
down to the river for a walk,
        just the two of us
with a flashlight, and ask him
        what the fuck
he is doing, *don't you know*
        what you are doing
will get you into trouble?;
        because he says *I know,*

I know and sounds sad
    the way a man being
reprimanded for trying to help
    those less fortunate
than himself sounds sad;
    because he knows
what's coming, what's always
    been coming — it is
just a matter of time before it
    comes and takes
all that he has built away;

1994

Because the room is a campsite
    near Vancouver, BC,
where you meet D. for the first time;
    because he's the first
sane person you've met all summer;
    because he is a genuinely
nice person, a desert child
    from Southern
California, and you love how
    blown away he is by
the sight of trees beside blue water,
    the Northern Pacific
pushing into the coast, the cool inlets
    peppered with green
islands, bristling with pine trees
    as tall as buildings;
because D. is completely non-toxic,
    pure in his happiness
to be here, to spend a year
    in Cape Breton with Don
and the other students we plan
    to pick up on the way
back to Nova Scotia; because he saw
    Don's ad in a home-
schooling magazine and asked
    his mother if he could go;
because all he'd wanted
    for years was to go back
to Indiana, the most beautiful place
    he'd ever seen, because
of the trees; because I've finally made
    a friend, and I can't wait
to show him the best spots in the
    woods near Don's place;

because we promise each other
        we're totally gonna
hang out this year, and in my mind
        I'm already convincing
my mother to drive me to the island
        more often, once a
month at least; because an hour
        after we meet we're
already planning to build a fort,
        and two days later,
after a fight breaks out, we ditch
        the idiots and follow
the train tracks until a train
        comes, about a mile
from where we've pitched our tents,
        and dare each other
to stand close enough to feel
        the train's vacuum
as it whips past us, opening
        our arms to its tremendous
creaking power, screaming
        until the last car
clatters past us;

Because the room is an airless
    classroom in a school
with no windows where a voice
    calls your name over
the PA so everyone assumes
    you're in trouble;
because it is French class, fifth
    period, and it's your
mother on the phone, wanting
    to know if you've heard
from Don, but not telling you
    why she wants to know,
telling you *I'll tell you later*
    and *I just need to know*
where Don might go —
    though why would you?
Don doesn't call you, you can't
    remember a single
occasion on which either of you
    talked by phone;
because *you knew him better*
    than anyone, she says;
because the truth is clear even if
    the logistics aren't,
it's so obvious what happened:
    somebody held on
to the feather, kept talking;

Sydney, 1994 – Fall

Because the room is a Motel 6
where three boys
are waiting for Don to finish
his meeting or was it
his dental appointment?; because
the story keeps changing
every hour that he calls to keep
them calm and patient
and make them wait without
wandering — *just a few more*
hours he tells them, *things are*
a little more complicated
than I thought; because the boys
get restless and one of
them is old enough to be
suspicious, *something*
is wrong he says, *something isn't*
right, so he calls
the desk manager, who calls
the police, who want
to file a missing person report;
because a day has passed
into night and night into
morning and Don has still
not returned, has stopped
calling even; because
the only number the oldest boy
knows to call is mine,
so the police reach my mother,
who calls me at school,
wanting to know where Don is
and where he might
have gone; because there is no
chain of custody —

all three boys are foreign citizens
        and must be returned
immediately to their countries
        of origin — and my mother,
being a responsible woman,
        a parent of three,
drives three and a half hours
        northeast to Sydney,
at the lung tip of Cape Breton
        Island, to fetch the boys
while the RCMP contact
        Immigration who liaise
with New Mexico State Police
        and California State
Police and the U.S. Embassy
        in Saudi Arabia;
because plane tickets need
        to be arranged and
one of the parents doesn't have
        any money; because
the whole thing takes about
        a week, maybe longer,
so the two older boys and I
        drink stolen bitters
on my bedroom floor while
        the rules of adult
uncertainty roll forward;

Because the room is the men's
       room just outside
the teachers' lounge which has
       the cleanest seats
and I need to think about
       what's clearly going
to happen next; because all eyes
       will turn to me, *the one*
who knew him best, and there
       will be no denying
anything, unless . . . ; because
       my mind has been
trained to make exceptions, nothing
       is ever absolutely true;
because human beings apply
       their aberrations
unwittingly, inconsistently,
       judiciously; because
I can always say it didn't happen
       to me and who could
prove it did?; because I'll say
       I was the exception,
the one whose trust couldn't be
       violated — or rather,
better, it was my father whose
       trust even Don
wouldn't violate; because *that*
       will appeal
to my father's vanity;
       because my mother
will blame herself in parallel
       to everyone else;

because her blame will be
   obvious, will be a truth
impossible-not-to-accept;
   because I know
one day I'll have to come clean,
   but not yet;

Because the room is a letter
    addressed to you, in it he writes,
You were always the most important
    and gives his regards
to my parents and sisters,
    to my parrot, Max, who
crapped his fair share on my shoulders;
    because the letter says
All I'm taking with me is my wallet,
    a change of clothes,
and a photo of you, but admits
    to nothing out of the ordinary
beyond the simple fact
    that he had to leave
his students stranded
    at a roadside motel
outside Sydney, Nova Scotia,
    while his wallet, spare
socks, and a photo of me raced
    south to Halifax
International Airport in the van
    he abandoned seven
hours later when he boarded
    a plane to Boston,
and then another to Manila,
    though it would be
unclear whether he had actually
    gotten on it or not,
    and right now that doesn't
    matter anyway since
there is only one APB out
    for a *missing person,*
and everyone is worried for him;

Because the room is an abandoned
    cabin in a meadow
surrounded by trees and a river
    whose rush sounds like traffic
rising up from the deep ravine
    below us; because the
cabin is abandoned and no one
    knows how long it will
take to get ransacked; because
    my sisters and I want
to take what books we can before
    the damp consumes them all;
because it is fall, red and yellow
    leaves paving the path up
to Don's cabin one month later
    and we have no idea
what we will find there —
    What if it's been burned down?;
because parents are angry now,
    vandals are everywhere
and burning abandoned cabins
    is not an unusual form
of entertainment around here;
    because the cabin is
still standing when we get there
    with a padlock on the door,
so I break in through the basement,
    and race upstairs to find
what I am looking for before
    letting my sisters in
through a window; because
    what I am looking for
is no longer there, the closet
    and all its secret contents

have been cleared; because I say,
    Don's already been here
and prove it by pointing to the
    empty shelf where Don
kept nude photos of me and god
    knows who else, and say,
Don kept money here; because my
    sisters are here for books,
so we stuff as much as we can
    into our backpacks;
because we know that whatever
    we leave won't survive
the winter, first one window
    will break then another,
till the floor is covered
    in fallen leaves
and snow, until the books
    and upholstery are rotten
and the whole thing
    gets consigned to fire;

Because the room is the room
    in which you sit
with your friend drinking
    stolen beer; because
he is your neighbour, in a place
    that bores the shit
out of both of you; because
    bored boys do things
they shouldn't;
    because you get along,
but only after school when no
    one else can see you;
because neither of you has a girl-
    friend but you are both
horny and bored and you at least
    are curiously immune
to things that normally would
    have repulsed you;
because he is curious, too,
    and when you ask
to see his thing, he pulls it out
    and wags it in your face,
then asks to see yours, too;
    because his thing
is bigger than your thing,
    curves to the left
like a brown banana
    with a bulbous tip;
because yours is paler, smaller
    but only by a year
(or so you hope!); because he's
    been with girls before,
which makes you horribly insecure;
    because results are

all that matter and his splooge
　　is ridiculously huge;
because the minute it's over
　　you are right back
where you were, *fucking*
　　bored, and somehow
more desperate than before;

1996

Because the room is not a room
    but an entire country
I know nothing about except
    that *boys can be bought*
for cheap; because for years
    I have imagined Don
in the Philippines, squatting
    on a dirt floor
surrounded by dark-skinned boys
    smiling through
unbrushed teeth at one of his
    wondrous stories,
a story, perhaps, about a place
    where the water
is so clean one can drink it
    straight from the spring,
where it comes out almost sweet;
    because he is in a place
where rain tastes sweet but only
    because of the pollution
and for some reason I imagine him
    buying bracelets
from tiny boys with naked asses
    and callused feet;
because I saw it in a *National*
    Geographic, a hot place,
wild with opportunities for sex,
    where for a few dollars
parents can be bought,
    police officers can be bought,
children can be brought to you;
    because I imagine men
coming for Don in the night,
    gang men in dirty clothes

out to rob an old pervert
    out of his element;
because Don has no money,
    all his bank accounts
are monitored and his credit cards
    have been blocked;
because in my dreams he comes
    back — I am at the mall,
or in my bed, unable to push him
    away, my arms oddly
weak, unresponsive; because
    his beard burrows deep
into my crotch, *beard to beard*,
    he jokes; because I am
fully grown now, my body has
    finished devouring itself;
because being weak scares me
    more than anything;
because it isn't his strength
    that scares me but
his insistence and my inability
    to resist that
which is no longer irresistible;

1997

Because the room is a strip
        of land behind my house
where a girl and I plan to have
        sex for the first time
and she asks me
        if I've ever done it before,
ever worn a condom before,
        and I have no idea
what to say so I say,
        No, you are the first
then change my mind, say,
        No, well actually . . . ;
because I don't want her to think
        I'm a virgin, but
now I'm caught in the weirdest
        kind of lie — a lie
with two parts, both true:
        the *I've-never-fucked-*
a-girl-so-I'm-technically-a-virgin
        part, and the *I-fucked-*
an-old-man-up-the-ass-so-what-
            does-that-make-me-now
part; because the story I remember
        is not the story I want
to tell; because right now I only
        remember episodes
and they all gross me out;
        because what's interesting
is not the plot, but what happens
        once the story is over,
so I tell her about a woman
        I met in Mexico
when I was fourteen, an entomologist
        with tanned breasts

and hands like sandpaper, whose
            moans shook the grass
walls of our hut at the far end
            of the beach, whose
laughter broke with the waves
            and somewhere behind
the tree-lined beach, church bells;
            who said *cheers* and got me
drunk on red wine from a box;
            because this answer
is real enough to reassure her
            that I am still pure
but possibly a little warped,
            so she says, *ok,*
I figured there was a little something
            there, and blows out
the candle so we can start;

1999

Because the first adult you tell
    is your older sister,
and the result is hilarious;
    because she acts like
it's something that happened to her,
    even though the only
thing that happened was that
    you told her; because
now her eyes are full of tears,
    so you try to hug her
and she says, *No, don't, that's not*
    what I want, so you
change the story, find another
    thread of truth,
but the new version
    only confuses things further;
because she says, *Which one is it?*
    You were his lover or you
were abused?; because both things
    can't be true;
so she asks *Why?,*
    she asks, *How?*;
because everything I say
    comes out wrong,
and there's no one true story
    I can tell that will make
her go, *Oh, ok, now I understand*;
    because you're only
just now trying out the truth;
    because what's true
is the room you've shattered
    and must now piece
back together, but the shards
    are many and, admit it,

you don't have patience for puzzles;
    because something
incomprehensible just happened
    that actually happened
a long time ago for you;
    because even *you*
still have no clue, it would be easier
    to solve *Pi* than
crack the code of the man
    who molested you;

Because the room is a jail cell   *Main Street, 1999 – Summer*
    in Contra Costa, California,
where Don has been arrested
    and is now awaiting
extradition four and a half years
    after he escaped, and
no one blames him for being afraid
    of California prisons,
but charges are pending and
    more are on the way;
because within days
    Don is on a plane
to Nova Scotia, in a transport van
    to my home town,
the county seat, where he'll
    await trial in a red-
bricked jail behind a white-pillared
    courthouse two blocks
from the Chinese restaurant
    on Main Street
where my younger sister and I
    dare each other
to throw pebbles at his window
    to see if he'll look out,
to see what he looks like now;

Because the room is any room   *New Jersey Turnpike, 1999 – Summer*
        you can find yourself
alone in long enough to get
        yourself off; because
the room is a truck stop on I-95
        in New York State
with a grimy bathroom and dried
        piss on the seat;
because the smell kills your
        inspiration and you
try to get it done fast;
        because something
boils inside you — you can't stop —
        and you know
that as soon as you walk out,
        the urge will come back;
because the girl is fresh
        in your mind,
when she leans down you see
        her breasts, soft,
with a line below the shirt
        where her tan skin
whitens and for a moment,
        a nipple appears;
because when she looked up
        and caught you staring
she smiled; because all of her
        gestures are purposeful
now that she's in your mind,
        where you keep her,
and don't let her go, not until
        you let go, which
is taking forever; because now
        someone is knocking

on the door, *You alright in there?*
    Still alive?
so you give up, slide the lock,
    step outside,
avoiding eye contact, squinting
    into the sudden
brightness, and grope your way
    back to the car;

Because the room is a courtroom   *Main Street, 1999 – Summer*
          in Antigonish, Nova Scotia,
where Don fires lawyer after lawyer
          to keep himself out of court;
because the court grows impatient
          and orders the trial to start;
because subpoenas are sent;
          because you are a recipient,
a witness for the defence;
          because his wife loves him
and spends day after day
          in a lawn chair in front
of the laundromat staring up
          at the second floor
of the brick lock-up behind
          the courthouse where
he waits, third window from the left;
          because she *knows*
you love him, too, and begs you
          to testify on his behalf;
because *he loves you*; because
          he was your friend,
the only one you had, remember?;
          because she won't
let you forget; because forgetting
          isn't an option until
it's the only one you have left;

Because the room is the bar
   where you confess
to your father over a glass
   of single malt;
because he has ordered a single
   malt for you; because
he wants to know — or wants
   to know what it means
to know, wants to analyse it,
   to take it apart,
to make it acceptable;
   because he doesn't know;
because he thinks he needs
   to know more;
because knowing and
   understanding
are not the same thing;
   because facts are misleading;
because knowledge is a balm,
   but only for a second;

Venice Pizza, 1999 – Summer

Because the room is the liquorice   *Macken Road, 1999 – Summer*
     jar my mother foists
at me every time I look sad;
     because everything
that happens *now* is Don's fault,
     and therefore her fault:
if you can't sleep, if you sleep
     too much, if you break up
with a *nice* girl for no reason;
     because unlike my father
my mother doesn't ask questions;
     because the answer
to each one is the same, the worst
     possible explanation;
because my mother doesn't seek
     forgiveness
where absolution is unachievable;
     because the only thing
left to achieve are facts,
     and I can't watch her
face them, I have no answers
     to make her feel better,
and when I tell her
     it's not her fault,
that I don't blame her
     (*Don fooled everyone!*),
I realise the only answers she wants
     belong to questions
only she can answer for herself;
     because I can't help but
remember the long silences
     of our drives to Cape Breton,

to the petrol station where Don
    would pick me up, and how
I never once thanked her for it,
    barely said a word,
in fact, when all she wanted
    was to talk;

III

JERICHO

Because the room is a restaurant   *Philadelphia, 2003 – Spring*
      in Philadelphia
where my older sister and I sit
      waiting for our order;
because my sister is thinking
      about the children
she might have someday, and
      wants to know
if I will ever be a danger to them
      because of my *experience*;
because she is completely
      unembarrassed
by her bluntness, the presumption
      only an older sibling
can pull off; because her question
      is not really a question
but an assumption she expects
      me to refute (*of course not!*);
because it never would have
      occurred to her
had it not been for her friend
      (*we were just talking and . . .*);
because years later, after she's
      married, after her
daughter is born, I'll remember
      this conversation
and wonder if this is why
      she didn't let me know
until after they had gone
      they'd spent the entire
summer just a few hours' drive
      from where I was living;
because the world we live in
      is full of danger and risk;

because right now it is spring
    and neither of us
is married, neither has children,
    so the answer is easy —
I clink my bottle to hers and
    let the too-sweet beer
carry her doubts into my belly;
    because food is on the way;
because the answer she wants
    is the one I can't give her;

Because the room is a bench   *Vienna, 2005 – Fall*
    in the baroque square
where I sit with my father
    and his many questions;
because he wants to know how
    he didn't know, how he
could have been so blind
    to the friend he thought
he knew so well; because *some lives*
    are simply unknowable,
but how can that be true when
    truth speaks for itself?;
because he wants to know,
    or needs to know,
how to review the evidence
    for himself, so it starts,
and, strangely, I am happy
    to indulge him,
to let his questions structure
    the story, give it shape;
because my father is a man
    who probes for clarification
even if the details are more
    than he can stomach;
because it's still new to me, too,
    all this talking,
and my father is determined
    to remain detached,
above it, like a scientist studying
    the behaviour of a tribe,
and he wants to show me
    he isn't afraid
to get his hands dirty; because
    like every scientist

he operates from a hypothesis:
        the good family,
the educated family, the boy
        who was taught
right from wrong; because
        he wants to know how
his son could let something
        like this happen to him:
Remember when I quizzed you?
        when I told you
if anything ever happened,
        you wouldn't get into trouble?;
because it still hurts him
        to think that Don
didn't actually value his friendship;
        because for five years
I'd helped him believe
        nothing had happened to me,
that Don preyed only on boys
        from broken homes,
boys without fathers; because
        Don's desires obviously
weren't limited to a demographic —
        his *entire* business
depended on his friends;
        because my father
cannot tell me he is relieved
        his youngest daughter
was *spared*; because a daughter
        is safe, a father is also
lucky; because he doesn't yet see
        how his daughter was used
as bait for love-sick boys,
        as were all our sisters;

because, like most fathers, what
he had worried about most
was *her* ability to survive *us*:
our wild, unchecked
minds, our grubby hands;
because it was a *relief*
when summer ended and no one
came home pregnant;

Because the room is an unmade
        bed scented with perfume
and sweat and dirty sheets
        where you've awoken
from a dream in which Don
        has found his way once
again into your body; because
        once again you've failed
to resist the weight of his arms
        on your chest, his anxious
hands, his exploring mouth;
        because the moment
he lets you go you wake up fast
        and the woman next to you
wants to know what you were
        dreaming — *it's like you*
were drowning, she says, *like you*
        were stuck under water —
and for some reason you can't stop
        laughing, because it's true,
Don is like water to you,
        and so for the first time,
you decide to tell her *the truth*
        if only to make it true;
because to recount the myth
        of yourself is to destroy it:
so you start with the image
        of a boy in a loincloth
covered in war paint, holding
        a spear in one hand
and a medicine staff in the other;
        because his hair
is braided with feathers;
        because severed wings

124

are strapped to his arms;
      because there are others
in this picture, boys whose faces
      are obscured by paint,
whose names he cannot say;
      because one of them
holds the long, mottled feather
      of a young bald eagle,
you know it's his turn now —
      in this way, the myth
is ready: we had a feather,
      only those who held it
were allowed to speak;

ACKNOWLEDGEMENTS

My gratitude to the many friends who took the time to read this manuscript at various stages and offer their insights, critiques, and encouragement. There are more of you than I have space to name here. But I would be remiss not to mention the generosity, in particular, of Sara Peters, Natashia Deón, Jessica Mensch, James Mensch, Steve Hardy, Jakub Kučera, and Robin Elliott, for graciously letting me bomb them with multiple early drafts and responding to each with valuable and substantial advice.

My eternal gratitude, as well, to those readers of later drafts, whose insights and encouragement came at critical moments in the development of the book, especially Christopher Crawford, Kate Singer, Stephan Delbos, Donna Stonecipher, Michael Stein, Justin Quinn, Joshua Weiner, Stanley Plumly, Michael Collier, Keith Driver, Bradley Paul, Matthew Olzmann, Clare Banks, Michael Theune, Greig Sargent, L.S. McKee, and Ben Williams, whose questions and comments opened up new ways of thinking about the book I was trying to write.

Francesca Bell and Jan Zikmund deserve special thanks

for their great patience in reading each of my "final" drafts before I was ready to turn it in to my publisher.

Immense gratitude to my editor, Jill Bialosky, for her insights, and for believing in this book; and to Drew Weitman, for guiding me through the publication process with patience and élan. For their early and critical endorsements: Stanley Plumly, Michael Collier, Stephanie Burt, Donna Stonecipher, Ernest Hilbert, and Joanne Diaz.

A bow of thanks and acknowledgement to my teachers, who often went well beyond the call of duty to offer their support and encouragement as I was figuring out how to write, and whose friendship and generosity continued well past the expiration date of their responsibilities: Eleanor Mutimer, Richard Jackson, Greg O'Dea, Stanley Plumly, Joshua Weiner, Michael Collier, and Elizabeth Arnold.

Profound thanks to Antonín Lukeš for his many years of friendship and employment, and for giving me the time I needed to complete this book, even while I was being paid to do other things.

Finally, but always first, to my wife, Zuzana Sklenková —without your love and friendship nothing useful would have come of my life. I love you.

Note on the Chronology: While I was usually able to recall the year and the general time of year, I could not always recall the exact month when certain events took place. Arranging the scenes by season allowed me to organize the chronology in a way that was true to memory as I recalled it, and plausible in the light of facts that I was able to verify later.